Remember the Rock

by Philip R. Hastings

special thanks to Edward J. Brunner

edited by Walt Lankenau

ISBN 0-944119-01-8

ANDOVER JUNCTION
PUBLICATIONS

BOX 1160, ANDOVER, N.J. 07821

CONTENTS

ASSOCIATED ARTISTS
OF DIXIE

AJ-101

FRONT COVER: Train 10, the *Corn Belt Rocket* with 11 cars, slows for a stop at Grinnell, Iowa.

REAR COVER: The brakeman on train 190, the *Zephyr Rocket,* awaits the highball at Waterloo.

Remember the Rock

WHEN WE MOVED to Waterloo, Iowa in 1959, it was impossible to venture far from home without encountering one line or another of the Rock Island Railroad. They covered the state like a case of varicose veins. In fact, in 1946, over 27 percent of the 7650-mile Rock Island system was in Iowa, about equal to the road's mileage in both Kansas and Oklahoma.

The former Burlington, Cedar Rapids & Northern main line from Burlington, Iowa north to the Twin Cities of Minnesota ran through Waterloo. This line played host to trains 190 and 201, the *Zephyr Rockets,* which used the Rock Island from Minneapolis to Burlington, running through to St. Louis on the CB&Q. The train, with its pooled Burlington and Rock Island equipment, passed southbound through Waterloo around 9:00 each evening.

The first serious Rock Island photo I made was of train 10, the Omaha—Chicago *Corn Belt Rocket,* picking up mail on the fly on the main line at Malcom in 1961. A more extended venture in November, 1963 took me to the northeastern corner of Iowa to record the last runs of trains 103 and 104 on the Decorah branch. The typical Rock Island caboose used on this run, an outside-braced side door affair rebuilt from an old boxcar in 1940, fascinated me. In 1967, I purchased Rock Island caboose 17772 and moved it to the Mid-Continent Railway Museum in North Freedom, Wisconsin.

At 8:30 p.m. on March 28, 1964, the Rock Island baggageman and a taxi driver chat in the drizzle at Waterloo, Iowa. Train 190, the *Zephyr Rocket*, will arrive on schedule at 8:57.

The author and son Hugh watch the activity at the Mid-Continent Railway Museum from Rock Island caboose 17772.

So what was remarkable about the Rock Island? Well, it was a pioneer railroad system, based in the midwest, which grew out to Colorado, New Mexico, Texas and Louisiana. Its passenger trains, such as the *Golden State Limited,* ran with the best, and some kept running until the last. Rock people were a bunch of fighters, who perhaps overcame more adversities than most railroaders. The railroad died prematurely in the merger scramble— if the ICC had acted in a timely fashion, the Rock Island would still be with us as part of the Union Pacific system.

In these pages, then, warmly remember the Rock.
—Philip R. Hastings

The *Corn Belt Rocket* swings past the abandoned depot at Malcom, Iowa on July 3, 1961. In addition to a parlor-lounge and dining car, No. 10 carries a working RPO.

West from Chicago

Two nearly new GP7's painted in the intricate red, white and black Rocket freight "wings" color scheme bring an eastbound freight over the Grand Trunk Western at Blue Island, Illinois on May 4, 1956 (left).

The arrival and departure boards at La Salle Street Station list *Rockets* to Peoria and Des Moines as well as Colorado, along with the *Golden State* and a nameless "mail-passenger" train, on October 13, 1966 (right).

A gateman guards the entrance to track 7, where the *Golden State* is ready to leave for California (lower right).

In October 1966, trains 3, the *Golden State*, and 7, the *Rocky Mountain Rocket* were scheduled to leave La Salle Street at 11:30 and 11:45 a.m. respectively. Below, the car knockers have finished their work on No. 3 while the *Rocky Mountain Rocket* is still accepting passengers.

In an effort to offset its passenger losses, the Rock Island carried mail in piggyback trailers on the rear end of some trains. On May 29, 1970 a pair of former Union Pacific E8's brought train 7 into Joliet, Illinois two days before its last run, with a seemingly healthy load of mail behind the coaches. By this time, No. 7 ran from Chicago to Omaha, its *Rocky Mountain Rocket* heritage only a fond memory (above).

Bureau operator Larry Mongan prepares a set of train orders to be handed up to a passing freight. His CTC board, which controlled the environs of Bureau Junction, was built by Union Switch & Signal just after World War II (right).

Another fading vestige of the *Rocket* legacy was train 6, the former *Des Moines Rocket*. By the time of this June 24, 1978 photo, the train had been cut back to a Rock Island to Chicago run. Here, Bicentennial E8 652, painted at the instigation of the 20th Century Railroad Club, leads No. 6 past the junction with the Peoria branch at Bureau, Ill. (left).

The Omaha Main

Chicago to Minneapolis train 61, with four second generation diesels, holds the main at Wilton, Iowa to meet Extra 4705 East which the dispatcher in Des Moines has run "wrong main" around trackwork on the eastbound track. When Extra 4705 clears, No. 61 will continue on to West Liberty, where it will swing around behind the station and continue its run north on the former Burlington, Cedar Rapids & Northern main line to the Twin Cities.

The eastbound *Corn Belt Rocket* bridges the Mississippi at Davenport, Iowa on April 17, 1968. The vest-pocket streamliner carries a Santa Fe mail storage car, an RPO, and a coach, parlor-lounge and dining car behind its E7 cab and booster. The lower level of the Rock Island bridge carries vehicular traffic between Davenport and Rock Island.

A U25B and GP7 lead local freight Extra 228 East across the Cedar River bridge at Moscow, Iowa in December 1979.

Extra 228's steel bay-window caboose passes the depot at Durant, Iowa. A friendly but firm admonition to enginemen graced the west wall of the station, apparently intended to give Silvis Yard, 28 miles east, an opportunity to prepare for any motive power problems headed its way. The town was named for Dr. Thomas C. Durant, a builder of Rock Island predecessor Mississippi & Missouri.

The attractive brick depot at West Liberty marked the crossing of the Rock Island's Omaha line and the former Burlington, Cedar Rapids & Northern main from Burlington to the Twin Cities. The CTC board in the depot controlled the crossing and junction, as well as the Omaha line as far west as Iowa City. Above, an eastbound freight clears the former BCR&N main line on its way to Chicago.

Marengo agent-operator Earl C. Berry copies orders for train 7, the *Rocky Mountain Rocket* on November 19, 1966. The telegraph sounder remains, but is seldom used anymore (right).

January 26, 1970 finds Berry again hooping up orders to No. 7, but it's not the same. In 1967 the *Rocket* was cut back to Omaha and renamed the *Cornhusker*, and by 1970 No. 7 was just a nameless mongrel carrying piggyback flats and a caboose.

F7 127 and EMD re-engined (and re-trucked!) FA1 142 hustle freight 83 west at South Amana on November 19, 1966. The through girder bridge crosses a Milwaukee Road branch line.

Rock
Island
MALCOM

The section gang reclaims the main for itself after clearing for the eastbound *Corn Belt Rocket* at Malcom on July 3, 1961 (see page 3). These men are charged with maintaining the track to 79 mph standards for the *Rockets* and fast freights (left).

The *Corn Belt Rocket* still looks healthy on June 26, 1964 as a trio of E7's bring the nine cars of No. 10 through the outskirts of Grinnell (right).

Four E units lead No. 10 across the C&NW (former Minneapolis & St. Louis) diamond in front of the Grinnell station on February 14, 1964 (below).

What a difference 15 years can make. On December 19, 1979 the railroad is on strike as supervisors bring Chicago to Denver freight 59 past the boarded-up station, GP38-2 4322, the *City of Herington* leads another GP38-2 and a U25B along a main line fraught with slow orders (lower right).

128 GP7's (including ten ex-Rio Grande units) comprised the largest group of a single diesel model on the Rock. Assigned to passenger, freight and mixed train service, most if not all served reliably until the railroad was shut down. Many were rebuilt by Silvis shops, Morrison-Knudsen and Precision National Corp. and renumbered into the 4400 series. Here, three examples just off an Iowa Falls local are on the engine pit at Des Moines in October 1973 (left).

Three solid maroon GE U25B's leave Des Moines Union—Fort Dodge, Des Moines & Southern—Chicago Great Western Junction with a freight, alongside an N&W job with an ex-Wabash F7 and GP35 on January 15, 1965. Legend has it that a Rock Island engineman coined the nickname "U-boats" for the big GE's soon after they were delivered (lower left).

A new bay-window caboose riding on unusual Rockwell express trucks follows train 44 across the Short Line Junction diamond, where the Chicago to Omaha main crosses the former St. Paul & Kansas City Short Line. The Short Line, built in 1911 to carry traffic between Manly and Allerton, was incorporated into the Rock Island in 1913 (below).

Slant-nosed E3 625 brings train 7 into Des Moines across the platform from the *Plainsman*, train 17 from Minneapolis to Kansas City, on March 1, 1968. The schedule allows ample time for passengers to make their connections.

SW900 558 has cut out train 7's snack-beverage car and some pig flats at Des Moines on April 28, 1969. No. 7 will continue on the Omaha with two E units, a baggage car, one coach, a mail storage boxcar, two pig flats and a caboose (above).

SW1200 933 trundles down the eastbound main at West Des Moines in August 1973. C&NW's former Minneapolis & St. Louis route from Fort Dodge enters Des Moines via trackage rights over the Rock Island main from West Des Moines (upper left).

A native red Rock Island E7 and a former Union Pacific E8 take train 10 past the Iowa State Capitol building and the Des Moines Union Railroad yards on April 22, 1970 (left).

Atlantic is typical of small towns on the Rock Island west of
Des Moines, with a sturdy railroad station and prominent grain
storage facility along the tracks. Former Illinois Central SW1
604, now Rock Island 4803, is based here to work the 25-mile
Audubon Branch on May 5, 1976. Track capacities at stations
on the branch are 31 cars at Brayton, 47 cars at Exira, 25 cars
at Hamlin, and 100 cars at Audubon.

The station at Stuart dates back to 1873, when the railroad
built a sixteen-stall brick roundhouse there. Train 44 passes the
ancient brick structure on May 5, 1976.

1940-built 628, still maroon and stainless steel at Council Bluffs on February 5, 1967, is one of five E6's on the roster. Only the 630 would be preserved after shutdown (left).

An A-B-A set of E7's leads train 1 into Nebraska over the Missouri River bridge at Omaha on March 4, 1968. The mail and express-only remnant of overnight Rock Island service between Chicago and Omaha arrives in the early morning (above).

The *Corn Belt Rocket* winds through the maze of track at CRI&P Junction in Omaha on March 4, 1968 behind E3 625 and E7B 604. One E3 spotting feature which is apparent in this view is the roofline taper at the rear of the carbody, which was originally intended to blend the locomotive into the low profile of the following streamlined cars. Such esthetic niceties are academic at this point in 625's career, as the presence of Flexi-Vans behind the power suggests (left).

Train 59, westbound for Denver with an unusual (for Rock Island!) set of matched power, passes the former Omaha Union Station. The units are named *Glenn L. English* (4313), *Charles O. Laverty* (4317), and *City of Blue Island* (4329).

THE JOINTLY OPERATED Rock Island/Milwaukee Road tower at West Davenport, Iowa had always been known as "West Dav," though the dispatcher simply called it "WN". Once, an actual tower had been located here, but "cabin" would more accurately describe the structure which occupied the site in later years. Measuring perhaps eight by 15 feet, three men would be uncomfortably crowded inside. The third trick operator who worked there in 1976, a college graduate, never quite got over the conditions under which he had to work. "Primitive?" he would say. "The only way this place could get more primitive is if they took off the roof!"

The operator controlled only three electric switches. Two comprised a trailing crossover between the Rock's double-track mains, and the other was a turnout off the eastbound main. West Dav's modest plant made it look like a "retirement job", but the simplicity of the layout was deceptive. In truth, West Dav stood at an awesome bottleneck where up to 20 trains an hour might roll past at certain times of day.

About a mile east of WN at Missouri Division Junction, Rock Island's Kansas City line joined the Omaha main. While the Des Moines dispatcher controlled the junction, trains had to call WN for signals. Milwaukee Road trains from Chicago and Minneapolis to Kansas City shared the Rock Island main for 26.4 miles from WN to DY (Culver Tower, Muscatine, Iowa). They left the Milwaukee at Savanna, Illinois, running over the Davenport, Rock

West Davenport

Not much bigger than a relay box, West Dav Tower squats alongside the westbound main. Operator Fred Steenbock passes an order to Milwaukee Road train 242, about to diverge from the RI onto the DRI&NW to Clinton.

Island & North Western to West Dav, where they attained Rock Island rails via the turnout off the eastbound main. The Rock also had trackage rights over the DRI&NW to Clinton, Iowa. Since the DRI Line was unsignalled, all movements needed a set of train orders to run the 35 miles between West Dav and Clinton.

Rock Island's West Davenport Yard was not far from West Dav. In fact, the yard lead crossed the DRI&NW, which required Rock Island switchers to call for a signal every time they approached the DRI Line. To add to yard-related congestion, Milwaukee's Nahant Yard was a scant two miles west of West Dav, and each of the three daily Milwaukee trains each way stopped to

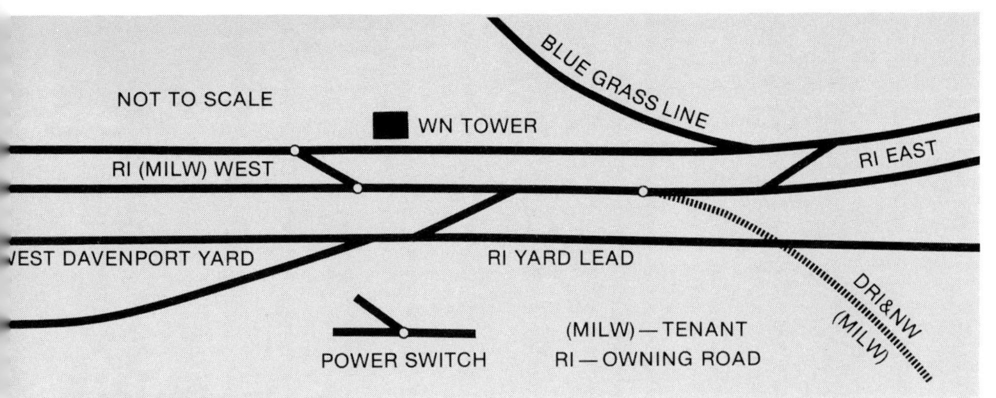

change crews, if not to pick up or set out, blocking one or both mains.

In addition to the mainline activity at WN, the old Burlington, Cedar Rapids & Northern "Blue Grass" line wandered off into the weeds behind the tower. This line once extended north to Cedar Rapids, but was cut back to a spur in the 1930's. The old branch retained its BCR&N heritage in one fascinating regard: it was a subdivision handled by crews out of Cedar Rapids. The Rock Island's daily West Dav to Clinton local worked the branch, and the crew had to be called out of Cedar Rapids and be paid deadhead time (at least 100 miles one way) because that was part of the original union agreement. Everyone wanted to work the Clinton local, and the seniority it took to hold that job guaranteed that everyone on it had white hair or long ago lost most of it.

With trains appearing from all directions, the objective at West Dav was simply to quickly run whoever showed up first. Priorities meant nothing. A Milwaukee switch engine was as hot as a Rock Island freight, because until it was moved, that switcher tied up the plant. The operator's main task was to identify who was showing up at the plant.

All this traffic required an intricate communication system. Because the Rock Island radio was packed with a steady stream of chatter from Silvis Yard, only ten miles away, a bell system was used. When the Rock's hot L.A. bound reefer train 01 went by the BN operator at 28th St. Crossing across the Mississippi in Illinois, he rang a certain signal in West Dav. The bell had the same pitch as a tricycle bell, and it was rung by twisting a crank a full turn for a long and a quarter turn for a short.

If the Milwaukee's Nahant Yardmaster needed to warn West Dav that an eastbound job was leaving or a switch engine was heading up to the Crescent Bridge, he had another set of rings for that. Crescent Birdge and West Davenport Yard were on the system, too, though they rarely had a chance to use it.

When a Rock Island eastbound approached, a strict sequence was to be followed; a shout into the dispatcher's phone to get a signal at Missouri Division Junction, a fast telephone call to the Government Bridge over the Mississippi (which could open for barge traffic but the op hoped it wouldn't), and a few turns of the crank to signal 28th Street Crossing that a train was on the way. The telephone, it was true, was always available, but a turn of the crank was faster and slicker.

How old was the bell system? The first-trick operator, a thirty-year man, said it had been in place long before he arrived, and it once included the old tower at Missouri Division Junction. Sometimes the system broke down; an extra board man might forget what to do, or the line would be cranked frantically for several seconds, which meant that the operator had to get on an open phone line and actually speak. Of course, that was playing outside the rules, a holdover from telegraph days, when no one had a direct telephone line. Transmitting messages by shorthand code was an anachronism even on the Rock Island, but the Davenport area system functioned as efficiently in the 1970's as the day it was introduced.

Despite the congestion and antiquated equipment, the men of West Dav Tower got the job done. Working there was quite an experience.
—EDWARD J. BRUNNER

Operator Steenbock at work in the confines of West Davenport Tower. The small CTC board controlled the junction between the Rock Island and the DRI Line.

The Golden State Route

Culver Tower in Muscatine marked the west end of the 26.4 miles of joint trackage out of West Dav. The Milwaukee tracks curve out of the picture behind the tower, which was closed in 1977 after the railroads agreed to extend the joint trackage to Polo, Mo., allowing the MILW to downgrade its line between those points to branchline status. This agreement was terminated by the Rock Island in May, 1978 after the Federal Railroad Administration placed unacceptable conditions on loans to the Rock for upgrading its track to handle the increased traffic. After the Rock's demise, the Milwaukee returned, and today this is the Soo Line.

MILW Extra 1511 West, detouring over the Rock on October 18, 1973 holds the main at Cotter as the conductor gets instructions (below).

Train 20 roars out of the sunset at Ainsworth behind a pair of UP GP9's, a Rock Island U25B and a P&LE U28B on October 18, 1973 (above).

Bright red GE U30C 4596 leads two older U-boats and a pair of GP40's across the Des Moines River bridge at Eldon with Dallas to Chicago train 20 on June 4, 1978. The 195-ton U30C's were the Rock's heaviest locomotives. Consequently, they were restricted to running only over the better-maintained main lines and in pools with other railroads.

Five passengers wait on the platform of the unremarkable Fairfield station as train 3, the extra fare *Golden State Limited* arrives from the east behind three somber maroon E units on June 12, 1967.

The *Plainsman,* train 17 from Minneapolis, has just arrived at Kansas City, Mo. behind E8 644 and E7B 607. It's 9:15 p.m. on March 1, 1968, and parcel post still accounts for a large share of passenger revenues, judging by the loaded baggage carts (right).

Former **EMD** demonstrator 952, now Rock Island 643, leads two sisters on the eastbound *Golden State* at Fairfield on January 25, 1968.

At dusk, the *Plainsman*, bound for Kansas City from Minneapolis, pauses for passengers at Allerton on March 1, 1968. Allerton is the junction of the Twin Cities line and the Golden State route.

The BCR&N Main

F7 104 leads freight 99 past the Quaker Oats plant and on into the Cedar Rapids yard. This 1966 view looks south from the passenger station platform.

West Liberty marks the junction of the Burlington, Cedar Rapids & Northern main line in the foreground and the original Rock Island Chicago to Omaha main line. Here, the blue GP38-2's of Extra 4341 West swing off the Omaha main and around behind the station to continue to Cedar Rapids on the old BCR&N. The Rock Island purchased the entire BCR&N in the summer of 1903.

Having just delivered a transfer run to the Burlington Northern, GP7 1257 returns caboose light along the waterfront to the Rock Island's Burlington yard to tie up for the night. The former Burlington Route main line crosses the wide Mississippi on the long through truss bridge in the distance (above).

Mediapolis, 15.2 miles from Burlington, makes do with a modest station, obviously converted from an old steel boxcar, alongside a small grain elevator. Passenger trains do not stop between Burlington and Columbus Jct.

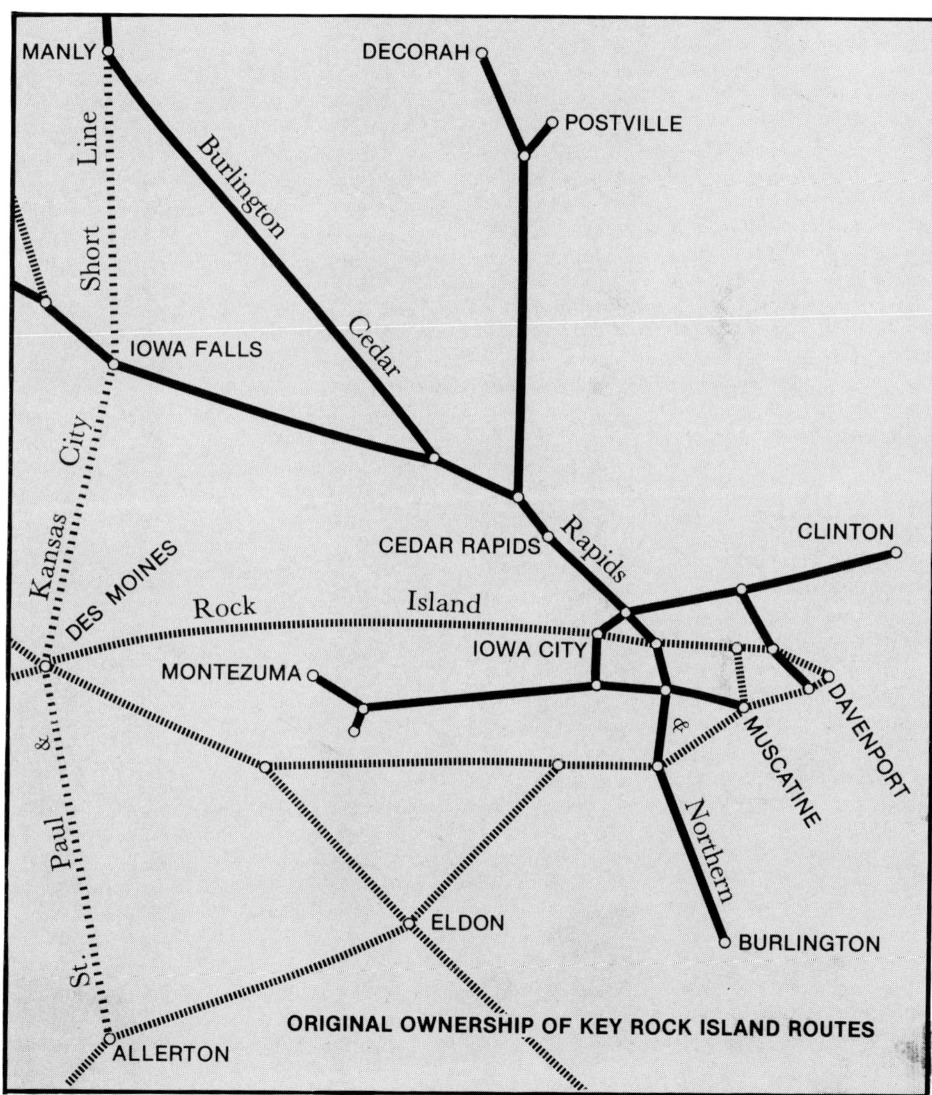

A westbound train of grain hoppers follows first- and second-generation road switchers along the Cedar River at Cedar Rapids in December 1979. 4453 was rebuilt by Precision National from GP7 1217 at their Paducah, Ky. shop.

Action at LaPorte City: A pair of striped F2's spliced by an anonymous F7 bring train 99 across Wolf Creek on September 10, 1964. 99 will set off those Rath refrigerators a few hundred yards ahead at the Waterloo Railroad (ex-Waterloo, Cedar Falls & Northern) interchange for delivery to the Rath meat packing plant (above).

A few days later, on September 17, operator Marvin Van Gorp hands up "19" orders to the engineer on the single F7 of Extra 675 East (left). Then, Van Gorp gives a set of messages to Extra 675's conductor aboard his classic Rock Island outside-braced wooden caboose as the section gang waits for the train to clear (right).

Burlington and Rock Island equipment is pooled between Minneapolis and St. Louis on the jointly-operated *Zephyr Rockets*. Below, silver Burlington E7 9935A rests during train 190's 20-minute station stop at Waterloo on March 28, 1964. The two baggage cars and single RPO attest to the amount of mail and express that is being handled on this cold night's run.

Train 190 awaits the highball at Waterloo on the evening of August 27, 1966 (above). The *Zephyr Rockets* are somewhat schizophrenic trains. In addition to the identity crisis brought on by pooled equipment, each train changes numbers twice between end points. Starting from the Twin Cities, the *Zephyr Rocket* is a southbound on the Rock Island's Des Moines Division, bearing the odd number 19. At Manly, the train enters the Illinois Division, where it becomes an eastbound, according to the timetable. By simply appending a zero to the train's original number, odd-numbered southbound 19 becomes even-numbered eastbound 190. At Burlington, Rock Island 190 becomes eastbound CB&Q train 8 for the remainder of its run to St. Louis. Northbound, the same logic applies. Burlington train 15 becomes Rock Island 201, which loses its "1" upon entering the Des Moines Division to become train 20.

On April 8, 1967, its final day of operation, *Zephyr Rocket* 201 scuffles into Cedar Falls behind E7 635. The attractive brick railroad station later became a restaurant (opposite).

MAIN ST
ST
Rock Island
CEDAR FALLS
US MAIL
6135

Train 62's extra, consisting of plow 95597, GP38-2 4311, SD40-2 4799 and U25B 217 runs along the Cedar River at Cedar Falls after opening drifts east of Manly on January 24, 1979. The snowplow, built on a former water bottom steam locomotive tender, is a pleasant reminder of old times. It is as distinctively "Rock Island" as the venerable wood cabooses (left).

GP40 371 leads a westbound freight across the Illinois Central Gulf diamond along the Cedar River at Cedar Falls, near the location where the snowplow is pictured on page 32.

Eight days before the end, train 61 heads across the West Fork of the Cedar River at Finchford, just west of Cedar Falls. On this March 22, 1980 the Geep has a future on the Missouri Pacific, but U-boat 209's prospects are not good.

ROCK
ISLAND
294
ROCK
ISLAND

The head brakeman of train 97 lines the siding switch at Shell Rock to let U33B 294 pull in for a meet with 94 on an overcast March 7, 1974. The sun is completely gone as SP U30C 7912 and a Rock Island U25B pull 94 by the hind end of 97, tucked safely in the passing track (opposite and top left).

With any luck, no thrills, chills or spills will befall The Greatest Show on Earth as it ambles south through the cornfields of Shell Rock en route from Minneapolis to Waterloo at 9:00 a.m. on August 9, 1971. Most likely, the ringmaster, clowns, lion tamers, aerialists and roustabouts aboard the 30-car Ringling Brothers & Barnum & Bailey Circus train are still sleeping off last night's show. Even so, FP7's 409 and 402 are a sight to delight children of all ages (top and left).

Zephyr Rocket 190 comes out of a summer sunset at Nora Springs, east of Manly, behind Burlington E8 9941B on June 28, 1964 (above).

Two weeks before the last run on this line, GP7 4544 brings Manly to Cedar Rapids local freight 196 into Greene. The abundance of grain elevators gives a clue to why Greene will become the headquarters town of Rock Island successor Iowa Northern (right).

The Kansas City Short Line

At Mills Tower, Iowa Falls, U30C 4589 and GP38-2 4334 are about to cross the ICG's Iowa Division with Kansas City to Minneapolis train 80 on December 22, 1978.

Relief operator Jeff Swartz has signals displayed north and south as he finishes copying a train order at Nevada. Extra 1356 North has just met Extra 4204 South, a ballast train headed by ex-Rio Grande GP7 5106 on August 22, 1974. The ten ex-Rio Grande Geeps are used singly, since they are not m.u. compatible with native Rock Island units. Five of the ex-Rio Grande units, including 4204, will leave the roster in the late 1970's, while the rest will be completely rebuilt, to the point of losing their dynamic brakes, in the Rock Island's Capital Rebuild Programs.

4204
4204

Branch Lines

This quaint trestle crosses the East Des Moines River at Armstrong, on the Albert Lea Branch. On July 17, 1968, GP7 1282 in maroon with a yellow nose treads lightly with Estherville to Albert Lea train 56. The classic consist of 40-foot steel boxcars and 10,000 gallon tanks is punctuated by a well-identified war baby wooden caboose (left).

Steel caboose 17877, built to the same general outline as several generations of wooden waycars before it, awaits a run at Estherville on July 17, 1968. The generous proportions of the brick depot hint at Estherville's onetime importance as a BCR&N division point. Four lines converge on Estherville: the Albert Lea Branch east to Albert Lea, Minn.; the Estherville Branch from Iowa Falls; the Worthington Branch west to Lismore, Minn.; and the Sioux Falls Branch west to Sioux Falls, S.D. The Worthington Branch extended as far as Watertown, S.D., at one time (far left).

The station at Dows, junction of the Estherville Branch and the Forest City Branch to Buffalo Center, nestles at the base of a towering grain elevator in a scene symbolic of the Rock's grain lines in northwestern Iowa (left).

GP38-2 4313, the *Glenn L. English*, returns to Des Moines with a Pella Turn on the Keokuk & Altoona Branch on December 19, 1979. Built as the Des Moines Valley and later reorganized as the Keokuk & Des Moines, this line was the first to reach the capital city of Iowa, in 1866 (right).

A pair of handsome *Rocket* Geeps bring Estherville to Cedar Rapids mixed train M924 into Traer on July 3, 1961. The arch roof combine, rebuilt from a twelve-wheel coach, provides both crew quarters and passenger accommodations on the hind end. The lack of on-board amenities and the eight-hour schedule for the 207-mile trip do little to encourage human patronage. The stately wood frame depot is slated for demolition, to be supplanted by the adjacent de-trucked doodlebug carbody rusting in the weeds. Ever resourceful, the Rock substituted old gas-electric bodies for large, outmoded station buildings at several locations including Avoca, Ia., Crystal Lake, Ia., Guthrie Center, Ia., Ellsworth, Minn., and Hebron, Neb.

Covered wagons to the rescue! F7 110 has been called from Cedar Rapids to replace GP7 1220, which burned out a traction motor on this westbound freight at Traer on April 8, 1963. The old station has been removed, and the remodeled doodlebug stands in its place. A wooden caboose brings up the rear of Extra 110 West, since mixed train service is no longer provided on the Iowa Falls Branch.

The Postville Branch is served by trains 103 and 104 out of Cedar Rapids. 103 leaves Cedar Rapids on Monday, Wednesday and Friday, returning on the crew's rest as train 104 on Tuesday, Thursday and Saturday. On a rainy June 25, 1968, an abbreviated 104 rolls past the brick ex-BCR&N station at West Union (left).

On a sunny day in September 1964, train 104 pulls in to Walker with a sizeable train behind its solid maroon GP7. The agent is handing his waybills up to the head brakeman, indicating that there's work to be done here today. After the switching is done and 104 resumes its trip home to Cedar Rapids, 24 miles away, the section crew can reclaim its railroad. Of typical wood construction, the depot reflects its BCR&N ancestry (right).

On the rainy morning of April 2, 1964, operator R.W. Brown hoops a "19" order up to train 104 at Center Point (below).

Cedar Rapids Yard is a focal point of local freight activity in northwestern Iowa. Wood and steel cabooses used on the branches to Postville and Iowa Falls are stored adjacent to the diesel shop (below).

1286
WALKER

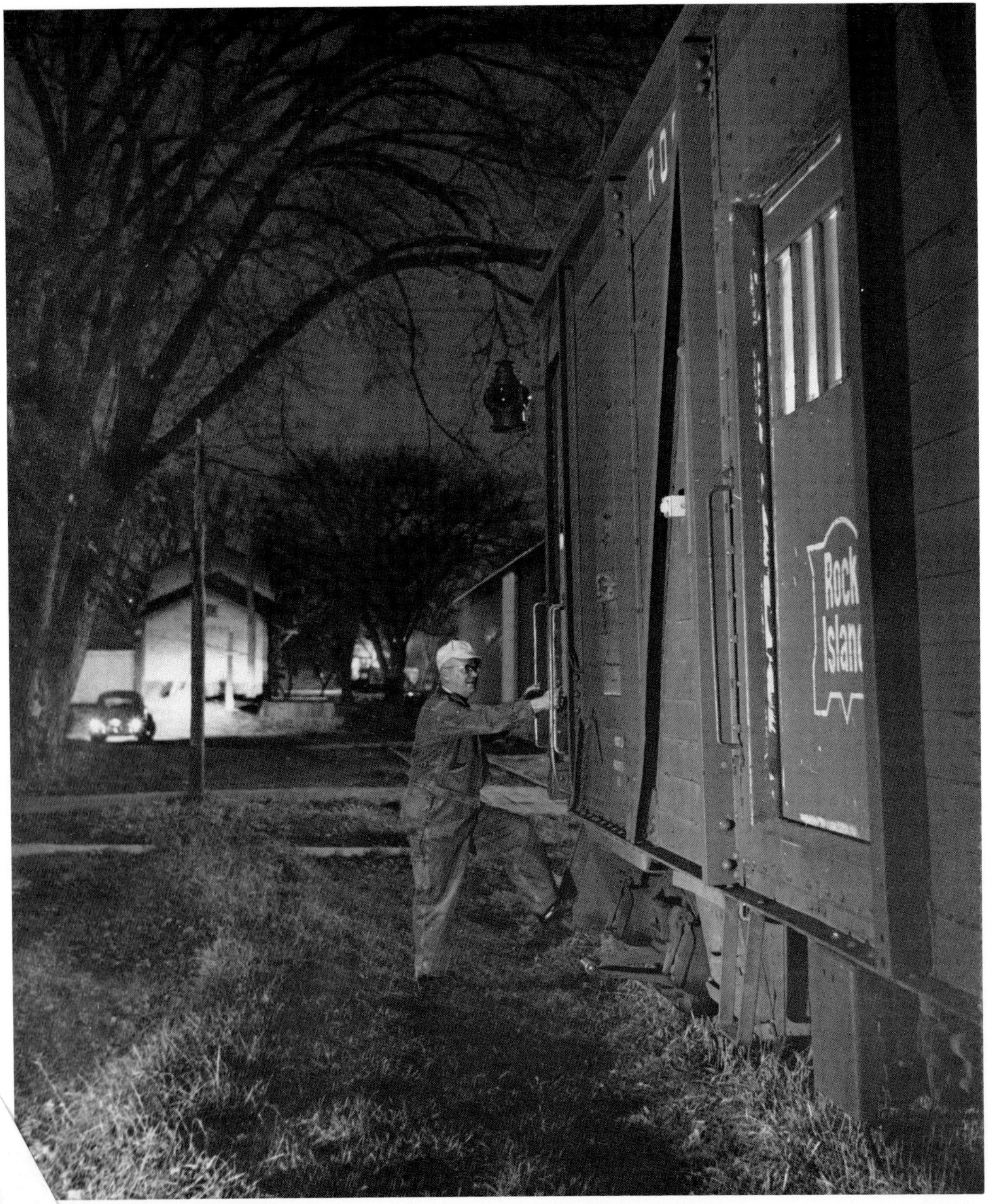

Farewell, Decorah

On a clear, cool Friday evening on November 1, 1963, conductor P.C. Wright climbs aboard caboose 17777 in the Decorah yard to get his rest after the day's run up from Cedar Rapids. This is the last time Wright and train 103 will tie up here; early tomorrow morning, he will highball the last departure of train 104 from Decorah (left).

Flagman Leo Hartman and conductor Wright watch as the Milwaukee Road diamond at Ossian, 14 miles from Decorah, clatters beneath 104's caboose for the last time. The smashboards will come down, the Rock Island rails will come up, and the Milwaukee will have Ossian all to itself (left).

Three miles from Postville, "Junction" will lose its meaning as train 104 leaves the Decorah line for the last time on November 2, 1963. GP7 1217 leads the short train consisting of mostly company service equipment. The Decorah turntable is loaded on the fourth car, and the old M of W passenger car recalls the days of mixed train service on this old piece of the Rock (left).

Decorah station stands silent as the train crew passes their last night here in the caboose spotted down in the yard. The venerable wood frame structure will survive as a private residence. It will also serve as a reminder of the Burlington, Cedar Rapids & Northern which built it around the turn of the century, and of the Rock Island which served it so faithfully, albeit unprofitably, for so many years (right).

Philip R. Hastings, M.D. 1925-1987

When I was growing up in Glover, Vermont, Phil's cousin Margaret was one of my best friends. She was determined that I meet her cousin Philip. She characterized him as being very intelligent, extremely interested in trains, and ''set'' in his ways. In the 45 years that I knew him, that characterization ran true!

He graduated from medical school in 1950, in spite of a growing family and taking time out for military service. He went on through extra years of training and became a psychiatrist, practicing until just two months before he died. In spite of the demands of his busy practice, his ''extreme interest'' in railroads continued to grow, becoming an obsession. Phil used every free moment and family vacation trip to visit and photograph his favorite railroads.

Many times, the family chafed impatiently while Phil waited beside the tracks for the one last chance to record a special event in the annals of railroading. He never made a big show of it, but his determination to record railroading as he saw it never ceased (he *was* ''set'' in his ways). And his thirst for recording railroads was insatiable; he always had one more picture to get, and then another photographic goal after that. It never ended.

Phil was exhilarated and thrilled by railroading, particularly by steam, and I am sure that in his part of heaven there will be a depot, tracks and trestles, and plenty of steam and smoke.—MARIAN B. HASTINGS, June 1, 1987